D1515498

Michael Owen

Tamra Orr

Mitchell Lane
PUBLISHERS

P.O. Box 196
Hockessin, Delaware 19707
Visit us on the web: www.mitchelllane.com
Comments? email us: mitchelllane@mitchelllane.com

Mitchell Lane PUBLISHERS

Printing   1   2   3   4   5   6   7   8   9

A Robbie Reader
No Hands Allowed

Brandi Chastain	Brian McBride	DaMarcus Beasley
David Beckham	Freddy Adu	Jay-Jay Okocha
Josh Wolff	Landon Donovan	**Michael Owen**
Ronaldo	Robbie & Ryan Play Indoor Soccer	

Library of Congress Cataloging-in-Publication Data
Orr, Tamra.
    MIchael Owen / by Tamra Orr.
        p. cm. – (A Robbie reader. No hands allowed)
    Includes bibliographical references and index.
    ISBN 1-58415-491-8 (library bound: alk. paper)
    1. Owen, Michael, 1979– –Juvenile Literature. 2. Soccer players–England–
Biography–Juvenile literature.
I. Title. II. Series.
GV942.7.O88 2007
796.334092–dc22
[B]
                                                            2006014812
ISBN-10: 1-58415-491-8   ISBN-13: 9781584154914

ABOUT THE AUTHOR: Tamara Orr is a full-time writer and author living in the Pacific Northwest. She has written more than 50 educational books for children and families, including *Orlando Bloom, Ice Cube,* and *Jamie Foxx* for Mitchell Lane Publishers. She is a regular writer for more than 50 national magazines and a dozen standardized testing companies. Orr is mother to four and life partner to Joseph.

PHOTO CREDITS: Cover–Karwai Tang/Alpha/Globe Photos; p. 4–Pedro Ugarte/AFP/ Getty Images; p. 6–Lutz Bongarts/Bongarts/Getty Images; p. 8–Philippe Huguen/AFP/ Getty Images; p. 10–Karwai Tang/Alpha/Globe Photos; p. 12–Bill Kostroun/AP; p. 14–Mike Hewitt/Getty Images; p. 16–Clive Brunskill/Getty Images; p. 18–Ross Kinnaird/Getty Images; p. 21–Scott Heppell/AP; p. 22–Sandra Behne/Bongarts/Getty Images; p. 24–David Benett/Globe Photos/Getty Images; p. 26–Ian Horrocks/Newcastle United/Getty Images

PLB

TABLE OF CONTENTS

Michael dances the ball down the field in the 1998 World Cup. His team won and qualified for the second round.

Soccer Superstar

The crowd held its breath. The opening match of the 1998 World Cup had just begun. England was playing Tunisia. Everyone was watching. They were sure Coach Hoddle would put Michael Owen into the game right away. Scouts from many different clubs had been keeping an eye on Owen since he was young. He was a great player.

Hoddle was not so sure. Instead of letting Owen play, he put in David Beckham. England won 2-0.

Next, England faced Romania. As the game started, Hoddle heard the people in the

Michael and Romania's Iulian Filipescu collide on the field during the 1998 World Cup.

stands. They were yelling Owen's name over and over. What should he do? Twenty minutes into the game, he sent the 18-year-old player in. The score was 1-0. Romania was winning.

When teammate Alan Shearer sent Owen a short cross from the right, Owen raced forward. He hooked the ball. He sent it right into the net. The game was tied! It was a great shot. Moments later, Romania scored again. They won 2-1. All eyes were on Owen now.

The third game began. This time England was playing Colombia. Hoddle sent Owen in right away. It was a good idea. Owen's excitement rubbed off on the other players. Two of them

7

Colombia's Mauricio Serna chases Michael down the field in the 1998 World Cup. England won 2-0.

scored a goal. Owen and Shearer kept the other team busy with fast passes and dribbles. England won 2-0. Already Owen was being called the "Boy Wonder."

The next game was against Argentina. Millions of people were watching to see if England could win this one. The game was close. Argentina scored the first goal. Next, Shearer got a goal for England. Then Owen took the field.

Getting a pass from Beckham, he raced past two **midfielders.** Next, he dribbled right around a defender. He kicked. He scored! His team ended up losing the game, yet fans all over the world knew the truth. Michael Owen was a soccer superstar.

In 2006, Owen attended the launch of England's new away uniforms. The new uniforms are designed like the classic 1966 uniforms, but they are made of a new type of fabric that will keep the players cool and dry.

Right from the Start

From a very early age, Owen loved to play soccer. He was born on December 14, 1979, in Chester, England. When he was little, he watched his father, Terry, play the game.

Terry was a midfielder. He had played for Everton and Chester. In 300 games, he had made 70 goals. He hoped his sons would like the game as much as he did.

Michael played soccer in his backyard and in a field near his house. He played with his brothers, Terry Junior and Andrew. It was not long before he was the best player, even though he was the youngest.

By the age of eight, Owen had his first coach, Howard Roberts, who was also the local gym teacher. He put Owen on the Under-10s team. Owen was small for his age. He looked

Michael remembers being a young soccer player like these kids. He often takes time out to sign autographs for them.

younger. He needed a note from his mother, Jeanette, saying it was okay for him to play.

In his first season, Owen scored 34 goals in 24 games as a **striker.** He was small, but he was tough. Sometimes bigger players gave him a hard time. He did not mind. He would get right back up and keep going. He was very fast. He almost danced up the field. He knew just where to keep the ball so that he could run without slowing down.

After one season, Owen joined the Under-11s. Everyone knew who he was. The way he ran and scored goals had been in all the local newspapers. At the 1990 Jersey Festival, Owen scored a **hat trick.** This brought his career total to a record 97 goals!

Owen's dad helped him be a good player. He taught him soccer skills. He also taught him to respect his coach and the other players. These were lessons Owen would remember.

Michael and Cyd Gray of Trinidad and Tobago both keep their eyes on the ball during a FIFA World Cup Group B match in 2006.

Here Come the Scouts

When Owen was 11 years old, he had already broken the record for scoring the most goals for his school. Scouts from many teams were watching him. Some wanted to sign him right away. He was still too young. Finally, Owen decided to join the Reds of Liverpool.

When Owen was 14, he went to a special soccer **boarding camp.** It was not far from London. He learned a lot about soccer there. He trained hard every day. At the same time, he worked with his team at their training

Michael battles with Liverpool's goalkeeper, Pepe Reina, during the 2005 game between Liverpool and Newcastle United. It takes plenty of hard work and physical skill to play soccer.

ground. He also went to school. He had to keep up with everything. It was not easy.

Owen was a great player. While he was on the Under-15 team, he scored 11 goals in just seven games. When the year was over, he had made more goals than any other player in his school's history. Next, he did something even bigger. He led his team in the **FA** Youth Cup. He scored a hat trick there. They won for the first time!

A few years later, Owen learned another lesson about soccer. He was playing against Yugoslavia. The team was rough. Owen was hit. He was pushed. He was bumped. The **referee** did not do anything to help him. Finally, Owen got angry. He pushed another player. The **referee** gave him a **red card.** Later, Terry talked to his son. He told him he had made a mistake. Owen was sorry. He learned that it is just as important to keep cool on the field as it is to play well.

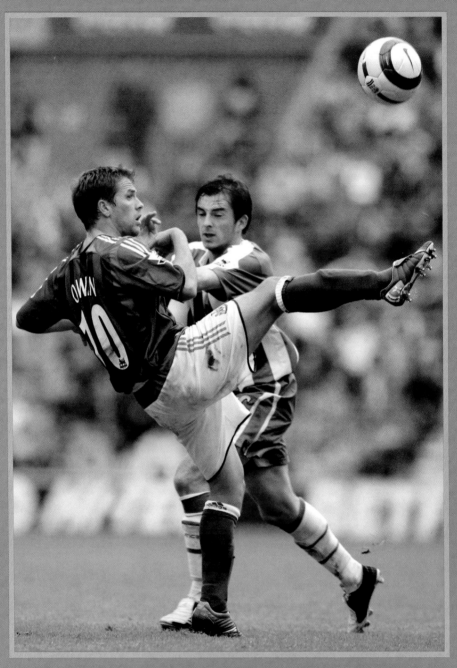

Michael sends the ball flying as Wigan's Leighton Baines looks on.
Kicks like this take a lot of strength and practice.

Years of Success

Four days after he turned 17, Owen signed a professional contract with Liverpool. Now he was a pro! A few months later, he played his first game against Wimbledon. In the first ten minutes, he scored a goal. Everyone was amazed at how well this young striker could play.

When Owen played in the 1997 World Youth Cup, people from all over the world became fans. He kept playing better. He even won the **Golden Boot** Award two times. He was given the Sports Personality of the Year Award. He was the youngest player to receive this honor. He was the top scorer in British

soccer, with 18 goals in 36 games. Not long after that, Glenn Hoddle, coach of the World Cup team, called. Soon everyone was talking about Owen!

Trouble was ahead, though. During a game, Owen hurt his **hamstring,** a large muscle in the back of the leg. It took a long time to heal. Owen missed seven games while he recovered.

Finally, Owen's leg was better. He was back out on the field. He was strong too! During a game against Germany, he scored another hat trick. When the Reds faced Italy in the fourth round for the **UEFA** Cup, Owen scored two goals. This sent Liverpool to the final. They took the title! In 2002, he scored his one hundredth goal for Liverpool. That same year, Owen gave an autographed Jaguar X-Type 2.5 sports car to the group Sport Relief. This group helps to raise money for poor children all over the world.

The next couple of years were good ones. During the 2002–2003 season, Owen scored

Thousands of fans welcomed Michael to the field in St. James Park after he signed a four-year contract with Newcastle. Helping him thank the fans is his daughter, Gemma Rose, born May 1, 2003.

28 goals. He led his team to the Worthington Cup championship. In May 2003, Owen welcomed his first child to the world, daughter Gemma Rose.

He had spent many years playing for Liverpool. Those days were about to end. There were some big changes waiting for Owen just around the corner.

21

Michael leans on Paraguay's Carlos Gamarra during the FIFA World Cup in 2006. Using the other team to help make a play is a slick trick.

Looking Ahead

Owen spent many years playing for the Reds. His last season for them was not a good one. He hurt his lower leg and had to sit out for a number of games. When he did play, he made mistakes on the field. He missed kicks. He did not take chances to score.

It was time for a change.

In 2004, Owen signed with Real Madrid. He did not stay long. Within a year, he was back to England. This time he was playing for Newcastle United. They paid millions of dollars for him to play. In one of his first games, he scored a **perfect hat trick.** This is rare! It

Michael takes time out to attend FIFA's 100 Best Players
event in 2004. Along with him is his childhood sweetheart
and the mother of Gemma Rose, Louise Bonsall.

means that he made one goal with his left foot, one with his right, and a third with his head.

In June 2005, Owen married Louise Bonsall. Then trouble returned during that year's New Year's Eve match against the Spurs. Owen ran into a player on the other team and broke a bone in his foot. The doctors had to operate and put a pin in it. It would take months before Owen would be able to play again. This was bad news for Newcastle. They wanted him to play in the World Cup finals that summer. The doctors were not sure if he would be ready or not.

Owen worked hard to prepare for the World Cup. He walked and ran miles each day. He hoped to return to the sport in April. He made it and entered the World Cup, only a few months after his son, James Michael Owen, was born. Unfortunately, in the second minute of a game against Sweden, his right knee buckled. He went down and was carried out on a stretcher. "As soon as it happened, I knew I was in trouble,"

With club staff Derek Wright and John Huntley watching carefully, Michael works out in the gym on his first day back in training for Newcastle United. He wears a cast on his foot while it heals from an operation in January 2006.

he said. "It was a major disappointment to pick up the injury so early in the game."

Even though Owen could not play in the 2006 World Cup games, he was there to cheer on his team. "I'll be following all the matches very closely and giving them my full support, hopefully all the way to [Olympic Games in] Berlin," he said.

Owen's years on the soccer field have taught him many things. One of the best lessons is to be there to support the team. Whether out playing on the field or recovering on the bench, Owen will be part of the game.

1979 Michael James Owen is born on December 14 in Chester, England.

1987 He gets his first coach and joins the Under-10s.

1990 He scores a hat trick at the New Jersey Festival. He signs with Reds of Liverpool.

1993 Owen goes to soccer boarding camp. He leads his team to win the FA Youth Cup.

1996 Owen signs a professional contract with Liverpool.

1998 He plays in the World Cup and amazes the crowd with his moves. He wins the Golden Boot award and PFA Young Player of the Year.

1999 He wins a second Golden Boot. He scores 18 goals, then injures his hamstring and has to miss the last seven games.

2001 Owen is named European Footballer of the Year and wins Golden Boot again.

2002 He scores his 100th goal for Liverpool. England again plays in the World Cup.

2003 He leads his team to win Worthington Cup championship. His daughter with Louise Bonsall, Gemma Rose, is born in May.

2004 Owen signs with Read Madrid; when he returns to England, he scores a perfect hat trick.

2005 Owen signs with Manchester United. He breaks his foot in a game against the Spurs. He marries longtime sweetheart Louise Bonsall in June.

2006 In February, son James Michael Owen is born. Michael Owen undergoes surgery on his foot. After training for months for the World Cup, he tears a ligament in his knee and misses most of the tournament.

boarding camp A camp at which people live for a period of days, weeks, or months.

FA The Football Association, the governing body of soccer in England.

Golden Boot An award given once a year to the player in each division who has the greatest competitive impact in the league.

hamstring (HAM-string)—A large muscle running down the back of the leg.

hat trick Scoring three or more goals by the same player in a game.

midfielder (MID-feel-der)—The player who helps the team by staying in the middle of the field to defend against a goal attempt.

perfect hat trick A hat trick for which one goal is scored with the left foot, one with the right foot, and one with the head.

red card A card given by the referee to indicate violent action on the field. The player is ejected from the game and may not be replaced, so the team is short a player.

referee (reh-fer-EE)—The person who enforces the rules of the game.

striker (STRY-kur)—A player in the forward position whose main responsibility is scoring goals.

UEFA Union of European Football Association, the administrative and controlling body for soccer in Europe.

Books

While there are no other books on Michael Owen, you might enjoy reading the following soccer biographies from Mitchell Lane Publishers:

Brandi Chastain	*Brian McBride*
DaMarcus Beasley	*David Beckham*
Freddy Adu	*Jay-Jay Okocha*
Josh Wolff	*Landon Donovan*
Ronaldo	

Works Consulted

ESPN Soccernet, "Owen 'Ahead of Schedule' in Injury Comeback," March 1, 2006, http://soccernet.espn.go.com/news/story?id=360304&cc=5901

"Men of the Week: Michael Owen," http://www.askmen.com/men/sports_60/68b_michael_owen.html

"Michael Owen," http://www.michaelowen.com.ar/michael-owen-biography.htm

Michael Owen biography, http://www.jockbio.com/Bios/Owen/Owen_bio.html

"Michael Owen Interview," http://www.wldcup.com/news/2000May/20000524_1465_owenmay_.html

"Michael Owen Interview," September 2, 1999, http://www.wldcup.com/news/1999Sep/199990902_2113_owenspark_.html

North East Wales Hall of Fame, http://www.bbc.co.uk/wales/
northeast/guides/halloffame/sport/michael_owen.shtml

Rudzki, Kyrstyna. "Michael Owen to Miss Rest of World Cup."
Associated Press, June 21, 2006,
http://www.wtopnews.com
index.php?nid=157&sid=799573

World Soccer News, "Michael Owen Interview," May 24,
2000, http://www.wldcup.com/news/2000May/
20000524_1465_owenmay_.html

On the Internet

The Official Michael Owen Fan Site
http://www.michaelowen-online.com

Jock Bio.com "Michael Owen"
http://www.jockbio.com/Bios/Owen/Owen_bio.html

Brief Biography on KidzWorld
http://www.kidzworld.com/site/p1893.htm

Road to World Cup 2006 personal blog
http://spaces.msn.com/worldcup-uk

Sport Relief
http://www.sportrelief.com

Multiple online magazine articles about Owen
http://www.michaelowen-online.com/news/articles.php